DATE DUE			

796.332   Cohn, Nate
COH   Los Angeles Chargers
c. 1 $19.00   10-2017

My First NFL Book

LOS ANGELES CHARGERS

Nate Cohn

www.av2books.com

LET'S READ
AV²
BY WEIGL™
ADDED VALUE • AUDIO VISUAL

Go to **www.av2books.com**, and enter this book's unique code.

BOOK CODE

T797634

AV² by Weigl brings you media enhanced books that support active learning.

AV² provides enriched content that supplements and complements this book. Weigl's AV² books strive to create inspired learning and engage young minds in a total learning experience.

Your AV² Media Enhanced books come alive with...

Audio
Listen to sections of the book read aloud.

Video
Watch informative video clips.

Embedded Weblinks
Gain additional information for research.

Try This!
Complete activities and hands-on experiments.

Key Words
Study vocabulary, and complete a matching word activity.

Quizzes
Test your knowledge.

Slide Show
View images and captions, and prepare a presentation.

... and much, much more!

Published by AV² by Weigl
350 5th Avenue, 59th Floor
New York, NY 10118

Website: www.av2books.com

Printed in the United States of America in Brainerd, Minnesota
1 2 3 4 5 6 7 8 9 0   21 20 19 18 17

032017
020317

Editor: Katie Gillespie
Art Director: Terry Paulhus

Weigl acknowledges Getty Images, Alamy, and iStock as the primary image suppliers for this title.

Library of Congress Control Number: 2017930839

ISBN 978-1-4896-5547-9 (hardcover)
ISBN 978-1-4896-5549-3 (multi-user eBook)

My First NFL Book

LOS ANGELES CHARGERS

CONTENTS

2 AV² Book Code
4 Team History
6 The Stadium
8 Team Spirit
10 The Jerseys
12 The Helmet
14 The Coach
16 Player Positions
18 Star Player
19 Famous Player
20 Team Records
22 By the Numbers
24 Quiz/Log on to www.av2books.com

Team History

The Los Angeles Chargers started playing football in 1960. They spent one year in Los Angeles. The team then moved south to San Diego. The Chargers joined the NFL in 1970. The team moved back to Los Angeles in 2017.

Barron Hilton from the Hilton hotel company was the team's founder.

The Stadium

The Chargers will play at Los Angeles Stadium at Hollywood Park. It is being built for the 2017 season. This will also be the home field for the Los Angeles Rams. The Chargers will play at StubHub Center until the new stadium is ready.

The Los Angeles Galaxy soccer team also plays at StubHub Center in Carson, California.

Team Spirit

The Chargers are nicknamed the Bolts. This is because their logo looks like a lightning bolt. The team had an unofficial fan leader while in San Diego. He was a super fan who dressed up as "Boltman." He cheered on the team from the front row.

Chargers fans dance to music when the team scores.

8

The Jerseys

The Chargers' jerseys were updated in 2007. The lightning bolt moved to the sleeves. The players' numbers moved to the shoulders. The Chargers mostly wear navy blue jerseys at home. They can also wear light blue jerseys for home games.

The Helmet

The Chargers' helmets have changed over time. The team now wears white helmets. The shiny white paint looks like metal. The team logo is on each side. The Chargers were the first NFL team to wear a facemask with a color.

The Chargers have worn blue helmets with white lightning bolts in the past.

The Coach

The Chargers hired Anthony Lynn as head coach after the 2016 season. He worked with six other NFL teams before joining the Chargers. Lynn worked with running backs for many years. He was also a running back in the NFL. Lynn won two Super Bowls as a player.

Player Positions

Gunners line up at the edges of the field during punts and kickoffs. Their job is to run down the field quickly. They try to tackle any player who catches the ball after it is kicked. The gunners usually play in different positions during other kinds of plays.

The Chargers played in the first NFL game outside the United States. It happened in 1976 in Japan.

Star Player

Philip Rivers joined the team in 2004. This quarterback set many records in 2016. Rivers scored 314 touchdowns by the end of that season. He made 176 starts in a row. That was the fourth-most of all quarterbacks ever. Rivers also holds team records for most regular season wins and most completed passes.

Junior Seau was one of the best linebackers of all time. Seau is in the Pro Football Hall of Fame. He went to the Pro Bowl 12 times. That is the yearly game for the best NFL players. Seau made 1,286 tackles for the Chargers. This is a team record. Seau was named NFL Man of the Year in 1994.

Team Records

The Chargers went to the Super Bowl for the 1994 season. Wide receiver Lance "Bambi" Alworth caught passes in 96 games in a row. He entered the Pro Football Hall of Fame in 1978. Running back LaDainian Tomlinson scored 31 touchdowns in 2006. That is an NFL single-season record.

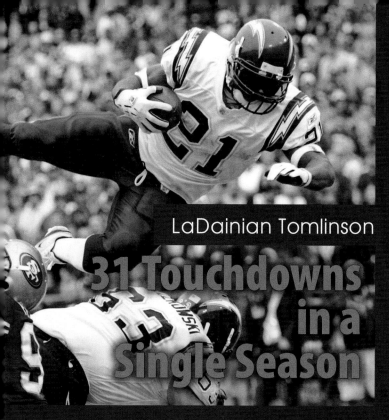

LaDainian Tomlinson

31 Touchdowns in a Single Season

Lance "Bambi" Alworth

96 Games in a Row with Passes Caught

1 Super Bowl Appearance

By the Numbers

Tight end Antonio Gates has been to **8 Pro Bowls**.

The Chargers have finished **1st** in their division **5 times** since 2004.

The team's record for scoring is kicker John Carney's **1,076 points**.

The Chargers' Hall of Fame has **39 players**, coaches, and managers.

Quarterback Dan Fouts threw the ball more than **4,000 yards** for **3 seasons** in a row.

Long snapper David Binn's team record for games played is **256 games** over **17 seasons.**

23

Quiz

1. Who founded the Chargers?

2. What is the name of the Chargers' new stadium?

3. What is the Chargers' nickname?

4. How many tackles did Junior Seau make for the Chargers?

5. How many touchdowns did LaDainian Tomlinson score in 2006?

ANSWERS 1. Barron Hilton 2. Los Angeles Stadium at Hollywood Park 3. The Bolts 4. 1,286 5. 31